# LOUISIANA

## The Pelican State

### BY
### JOHN HAMILTON

Abdo & Daughters
An imprint of Abdo Publishing | abdopublishing.com

abdopublishing.com

Published by ABDO Publishing, a division of ABDO, PO Box 398166, Minneapolis, Minnesota 55439. Copyright © 2017 by Abdo Consulting Group, Inc. International copyrights reserved in all countries. No part of this book may be reproduced in any form without written permission from the publisher. ABDO & Daughters™ is a trademark and logo of ABDO Publishing.

Printed in the United States of America, North Mankato, Minnesota.
022016
092016

THIS BOOK CONTAINS
RECYCLED MATERIALS

**Editor:** Sue Hamilton        **Contributing Editor:** Bridget O'Brien
**Graphic Design:** Sue Hamilton
**Cover Art Direction:** Candice Keimig   **Cover Photo Selection:** Neil Klinepier
**Cover Photo:** iStock
**Interior Images:** Alamy, AP Images, Corbis, Getty Images, Glow Images, Granger Collection, History in Full Color-Restoration/Colorization, iStock, Library of Congress, Louisiana Dept of Culture, Recreation & Tourism, Louisiana Dept of State, Matt Howry, Mile High Maps, Minden Pictures, NASA, New Orleans Pelicans, New Orleans Saints, New York Public Library, NOAA, Sugar Bowl, US Forest Service/Kisatchie National Forest, Wikimedia.

**Statistics:** *State and City Populations*, U.S. Census Bureau, July 1, 2014 estimates; *Land and Water Area*, U.S. Census Bureau, 2010 Census, MAF/TIGER database; *State Temperature Extremes*, NOAA National Climatic Data Center; *Climatology and Average Annual Precipitation*, NOAA National Climatic Data Center, 1980-2015 statewide averages; *State Highest and Lowest Points*, NOAA National Geodetic Survey.

**Websites:** To learn more about the United States, visit booklinks.abdopublishing.com. These links are routinely monitored and updated to provide the most current information available.

### Cataloging-in-Publication Data

Names: Hamilton, John, 1959- author.
Title: Louisiana / by John Hamilton.
Description: Minneapolis, MN : Abdo Publishing, [2017] | Series: The United States of America | Includes index.
Identifiers: LCCN 2015957607 | ISBN 9781680783209 (lib. bdg.) | ISBN 9781680774245 (ebook)
Subjects: LCSH: Louisiana--Juvenile literature.
Classification: DDC 976.3--dc23
LC record available at http://lccn.loc.gov/2015957607

# CONTENTS

# THE PELICAN STATE

**Y**ou can tell a lot about Louisiana by its history and its people. The state has an especially rich history. Its people are a wild mix from many different lands. This combination gives Louisiana a jazzy, let-the-good-times-roll spirit.

Louisiana is an important trade center. The mighty Mississippi River flows through the state and empties into the Gulf of Mexico. Many ships use the river to transport goods, making Louisiana a gateway to the rest of the world. In fact, more cargo tonnage is handled by Louisiana ports than most others in the nation.

Louisiana's location next to the Gulf of Mexico also brings great danger. Destructive hurricanes often pound the state. But Louisiana always picks itself up, cleans itself off, and looks to better times.

Louisiana is nicknamed "The Pelican State." Brown pelicans are often found on the beaches and waterways of the state's southern coast.

*Ships from around the world travel to New Orleans and other Louisiana ports to deliver and receive goods.*

# QUICK FACTS

**Name:** Louisiana was named in honor of Louis XIV, the king of France from 1643-1715.

**State Capital:** Baton Rouge, population 228,895

**Date of Statehood:** April 30, 1812 (18th state)

**Population:** 4,649,676 (25th-most populous state)

**Area (Total Land and Water):** 52,378 square miles (135,658 sq km), 31st-largest state

**Largest City:** New Orleans, population 384,320

**Nickname:** The Pelican State; The Bayou State

**Motto:** Union, Justice, Confidence

**State Bird:** Brown Pelican

**State Flower:** Magnolia

**State Tree:** Bald Cypress

**State Insect:** Honey Bee

Bald Cypress

**State Song:** "Give Me Louisiana" and "You Are My Sunshine"

**Highest Point:** Driskill Mountain, 535 feet (163 m)

**Lowest Point:** New Orleans, -8 feet (-2 m)

**Average July High Temperature:** 92°F (33°C)

Honey Bee

**Record High Temperature:** 114°F (46°C), in Plain Dealing on August 10, 1936

**Average January Low Temperature:** 39°F (4°C)

Driskill Mountain

**Record Low Temperature:** -16°F (-27°C), in Minden on February 13, 1899

New Orleans

**Average Annual Precipitation:** 59 inches (150 cm)

**Number of U.S. Senators:** 2

**Number of U.S. Representatives:** 6

**U.S. Postal Service Abbreviation:** LA

# GEOGRAPHY

**L**ouisiana is a Southern state. Its shape resembles a boot. Its "heel" and "toe" jut into the Gulf of Mexico. It shares its eastern border with the state of Mississippi. To the west is Texas. To the north is Arkansas. Louisiana is the 31st-largest state. It covers 52,378 square miles (135,658 sq km).

Louisiana is part of the Gulf Coastal Plain region of the United States. Its land is mostly flat. Elevation is higher in the north, then slopes gently downward toward the Gulf of Mexico. The state's lowest point is the city of New Orleans. It lies eight feet (2 m) *below* sea level. Under normal weather conditions, dams and levees keep the city from flooding.

New Orleans' levees could not stop the flooding caused by Hurricane Katrina in 2005.

New homes stand next to the rebuilt Industrial Canal levee in 2015 in New Orleans. Under normal conditions, the dams and levees prevent flooding.

ARKANSAS

Shreveport

**LOUISIANA**

TEXAS

*Sabine River*

*Mississippi River*

MISSISSIPPI

**Baton Rouge**

Lake Charles    Lafayette

Lake Pontchartrain

**New Orleans**

N

0          100 miles
0      100 km

GULF OF MEXICO

Louisiana's total land and water area is 52,378 square miles (135,658 sq km). It is the 31st-largest state. The state capital is Baton Rouge.

# Geographical Regions of Louisiana

West Gulf Coastal Plain

East Gulf Coastal Plain

Mississippi Alluvial Plain

The Mississippi Alluvial Plain runs through central Louisiana. It ends where the Mississippi River empties into the Gulf of Mexico. Alluvium is a type of soil. It is formed by sediments in river water, such as sand and mud. When rivers flood, they drop these sediments over the flat plain. The lowland floodplains build up over time. There are many swamps, marshes, and bayous in this part of Louisiana. Just off the coast are nearly 2,500 small islands. These barrier islands protect the coast from storms and provide shelter for wildlife, especially birds.

The West Gulf Coastal Plain is Louisiana's largest region. It occupies almost the entire western half of the state. Beaches and marshlands reach about 20 miles (32 km) inland from the coast. Gently rolling grasslands and hilly forests dominate the rest of this region. Driskill Mountain is in the north. It is Louisiana's highest point. It rises just 535 feet (163 m) above sea level.

The East Gulf Coastal Plain occupies most of the land east of the Mississippi River where it crosses Louisiana. It is mostly wetlands and low, rolling hills.

Important rivers and bayous in Louisiana include the Mississippi, Red, Pearl, Atchafalaya, Vermilion, Teche, Calcasieu, Boeff, Mermentau, Lafourche, and Sabine. The largest inland body of water is Lake Pontchartrain, north of New Orleans.

*Louisiana is filled with rivers, lakes, swamps, marshes, and bayous.*

# CLIMATE AND WEATHER

Louisiana has a subtropical climate. The air is often hot and humid. The average high temperature in July is 92°F (33°C). Winter temperatures are milder. In January, the thermometer rarely dips below freezing in the southern part of the state.

Because of its subtropical climate, Louisiana receives a lot of rain during the year. The state's average annual precipitation is 59 inches (150 cm).

Louisiana averages about 60 thunderstorms and 37 tornadoes each year. Because most of its land is low-lying, Louisiana is vulnerable to flooding from hurricanes. These large, powerful storms bring torrential downpours and high winds.

*Strong winds from Hurricane Katrina blew the roof off a Louisiana restaurant on August 29, 2005. The hurricane was the costliest natural disaster in the history of the United States. It was also one of the five deadliest hurricanes in United States history, killing nearly 1,000 people in Louisiana.*

In August 2005, Hurricane Katrina battered Louisiana. It brought winds of 125 miles per hour (201 km/hr) and flooded large parts of the state. Nearly 1,000 Louisiana citizens were killed. Hundreds of thousands had to move away from their homes. The city of New Orleans was hit especially hard. Years later, the hard work of rebuilding continues.

## CLIMATE AND WEATHER

# PLANTS AND
# ANIMALS

About 48 percent of Louisiana's land area is covered by forests. That is nearly 13.8 million acres (5.6 million ha). Pine forests dominate the

Longleaf pines reach to the sky in Kisatchie National Forest.

northern part of the state. Common Louisiana trees include oak, gum, magnolia, loblolly pine, shortleaf pine, slash pine, longleaf pine, tupelo, eastern red cedar, and black walnut.

The bald cypress is Louisiana's official state tree. It is a graceful tree that is usually bottle-shaped, with a reddish-brown trunk that is wider at its base. It has "knees" that stick out at the base, which are actually a special kind of root. The tree grows up to 120 feet (37 m) tall, with a trunk between 3 to 6 feet (.9 to 1.8 m) wide. The bald cypress has needle-like leaves that look like feathers. The leaves are shed early in the fall, which is why the tree is called "bald." The bald cypress grows well in swamps and other wetlands, and is often found draped in Spanish moss. It lives for a long time, sometimes up to 600 years.

An egret walks past cypress trees covered in Spanish moss in Louisiana's Atchafalaya Swamp.

Louisiana's state flower is the magnolia. It grows on the ends of magnolia tree branches. The flowers bloom in late spring and have a sweet fragrance.

Louisiana irises grow mainly in the state's marshlands. The beautiful purple, red, orange, and pink irises are Louisiana's official state wildflower. Other common flowers include jasmines, honeysuckles, azaleas, and camellias.

The black bear is Louisiana's state mammal. These large forest animals can grow up to 6 feet (1.8 m) in length. Adult males usually weigh up to 300 pounds (136 km), but some can weigh 500 pounds (227 kg) or more.

Other common Louisiana animals include deer, opossums, wild hogs, bobcats, minks, raccoons, skunks, rabbits, bats, nutrias, mice, and snakes.

The American alligator is the state reptile. They are often found lurking in Louisiana's southern swamps. The green tree frog is Louisiana's official amphibian. The honeybee is the official insect.

The brown pelican is Louisiana's official state bird. They were endangered for many years because of pesticide pollution. They have rebounded in large numbers in recent years. They hunt by plunge-diving into the water and scooping up fish in their large bills.

Other common Louisiana birds include wild turkeys, quails, ducks, bald eagles, hawks, owls, egrets, blue herons, and many others.

The official state fish is the white perch. Other fish swimming in Louisiana waters include catfish, bass, crappie, bream, gar, and more.

**American Alligator**

# HISTORY

Louisiana has a rich history. It has been ruled under 10 different flags since the early 1500s. Many people settled the area, including the French, Spanish, German, Acadians, English, West Indians, Africans, Irish, and Italians. But thousands of years before any of those people set foot in Louisiana, the land had been settled by Paleo-Indians. They were the ancestors of today's Native Americans. They built

Louisiana's Paleo-Indians built some of the oldest earthen mounds in North America.

communities. They hunted, fished, and grew crops. They also built large mounds of earth for religious ceremonies, especially burials.

By the time Europeans began exploring the New World, several Native American tribes had settled in today's Louisiana. They included the Choctaw, Natchez, and other tribes.

The first European to explore Louisiana was Hernando de Soto. He arrived in 1541, searching for gold. He failed to find any riches, and Spain lost interest in the Louisiana area.

In 1682, French explorer René-Robert Cavelier, Sieur de La Salle and his expedition paddled from the Great Lakes down the Mississippi River until reaching its mouth. He claimed all the land drained by the river for France. He named the new territory Louisiana in honor of King Louis XIV.

René-Robert Cavelier,
Sieur de La Salle claimed
Louisiana in honor of
King Louis XIV in 1682.

*Fort St. Jean Baptiste State Historic Site is a replica of the first permanent French settlement in Louisiana. It is near Natchitoches, Louisiana.*

In 1716, Fort St. Jean Baptiste des Natchitoches was founded along the Red River in northwestern Louisiana. Two years earlier, a French settlement had been established to trade with Native Americans. It was the first permanent French settlement in Louisiana. Today, a replica of the fort is a state historic site.

New Orleans was founded in 1718 by Jean-Baptiste Le Moyne, Sieur de Bienville. The city was named after Philippe II, the French Duke of Orléans. Its location on the Mississippi River, and its closeness to the Gulf of Mexico, gave it great trade and military importance. The city grew quickly, despite diseases and hurricanes. It became the capital of the entire French Louisiana Territory in 1723.

France was defeated by Great Britain in the French and Indian War (1754-1763). Instead of letting Louisiana fall into British hands, the French gave the territory to Spain in 1762. But only a few decades later, Spain gave the territory back to France in 1800.

*New Orleans crowds cheer as the United States flag is raised on December 20, 1803. The date marked the official transfer of the Louisiana Territory from France to the United States, following the Louisiana Purchase.*

In 1803, French Emperor Napoléon Bonaparte sold Louisiana Territory to the United States. The sale was called the Louisiana Purchase. At 828,000 square miles (2,144,510 sq km) of land, the sale almost doubled the size of the young country. The territory was later split into 15 new states, including Louisiana. On April 30, 1812, Louisiana was admitted to the Union, making it the 18th state.

*U.S. Navy forces captured the Confederate-held port of New Orleans in 1862.*

In the 1800s, Louisiana quickly grew into an agricultural powerhouse. Vast farms known as plantations produced cotton and sugar cane. Slave labor from Africa and the Caribbean helped make the plantations even more profitable.

When Abraham Lincoln was elected president in 1860, he vowed to restrict slavery. African slaves were so important to the state's economy that Louisiana joined the Confederate States of America, which broke away from the Union. This led to the bloody Civil War (1861-1865).

Union forces captured the vital Louisiana ports of New Orleans and Baton Rouge in 1862. By controlling the Mississippi River, the Union choked off many of the South's trade routes. By 1865, the Confederacy had lost the war.

After the Civil War, Louisiana's economy lay in shambles. Rich plantation owners lost their lands. Many average people could only afford to rent land to farm. They were called sharecroppers. Resentment against freed slaves and Northern political interference gave rise to racist groups such as the Ku Klux Klan.

In the 20th century, Louisiana's economy finally improved. New railroads helped the lumber industry. The oil and natural gas industries brought new jobs. Service industries also helped the economy.

Louisiana faced many challenges in the 2000s, including Hurricane Katrina in 2005 and the offshore Deepwater Horizon oil spill in 2010. Rebuilding will take many years, but Louisiana's spirit always seems to find a way to bounce back.

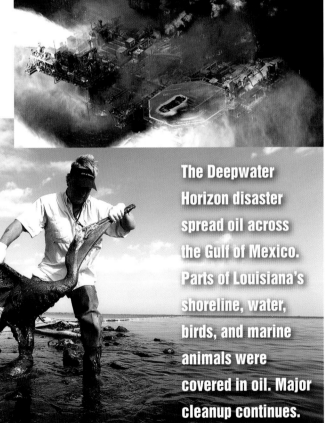

The Deepwater Horizon oil rig exploded on April 10, 2010.

The Deepwater Horizon disaster spread oil across the Gulf of Mexico. Parts of Louisiana's shoreline, water, birds, and marine animals were covered in oil. Major cleanup continues.

# DID YOU KNOW?

- The Lake Pontchartrain Causeway is the longest bridge over water in the world. It crosses Lake Pontchartrain, which is north of New Orleans, for about 24 miles (39 km). The causeway is actually two one-way bridges that are side-by-side. The first bridge was constructed in 1956. The second opened in 1969. They are supported by 9,500 concrete pilings. There is a drawbridge about halfway across that can be raised to allow large ships to pass.

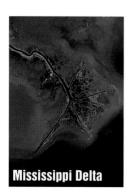

Mississippi Delta

- In the past, the Mississippi Delta (at the mouth of the river) grew larger each year. Today, much land is instead lost to the waters of the Gulf of Mexico. There are several reasons for this erosion. They include artificial dams and levees, rising sea levels, as well as the digging of canals and the draining of swamps for mining and logging. Louisiana loses about 29 square miles (75 sq km) of wetlands each year to erosion.

- In Louisiana, a person with dentures who bites someone can be charged with aggravated battery. The false teeth are considered a deadly weapon.

- South-central Louisiana is called "Cajun Country." It was settled by French-speaking people from Canada. Many Cajuns today speak a unique French dialect, and their spicy food and toe-tapping music are very popular. Cajuns have a long and fascinating history. In the 1600s, French colonists settled the province of Acadia (today's Nova Scotia, Canada). Great Britain soon took over the land. In the 1750s, many Acadians fled their homeland to avoid war between Great Britain and France. A large number found their way to French-speaking Louisiana, where they were welcomed. They farmed along the Mississippi River and the bayous of southern Louisiana. Many fishing villages sprang up in the swamplands. In the French language, Acadian is pronounced *A-ca-jan*. The newcomers were called "Cajuns" for short, and the name stuck. Today, the ancestors of the original Acadians can be found in communities along the Louisiana coast and in the central part of the state. This region is often called "Acadiana," or "French Louisiana."

- Baton Rouge's 34-story capitol building is the tallest state capitol building in the United States. It stands 450 feet (137 m) tall. Constructed in the early 1930s with Alabama limestone and Minnesota granite, the capitol is decorated with many sculptures and reliefs.

# PEOPLE

**Louis Armstrong** (1901-1971) was a jazz trumpeter, singer, and composer. His unique vocal style and daring trumpet playing catapulted him to fame starting in the 1920s. He was born and grew up in New Orleans, where he first learned to play trumpet. He was so poor he left school in fifth grade to collect junk and deliver coal. After succeeding in the jazz music scene, he played in some of the biggest clubs in Chicago, Illinois, New York City, New York, and Los Angeles, California. His records sold in the millions. Some of his most famous recordings included "Stardust," "Hello Dolly," "La Via En Rose," and "What a Wonderful World."

**Terry Bradshaw** (1948- ) played quarterback for the Pittsburgh Steelers in the National Football League (NFL). He led the team to four Super Bowl titles for the 1974, 1975, 1978, and 1979 seasons. He also won eight AFC Central Championships. Bradshaw was born in Shreveport, Louisiana, and spent most of his childhood in the state. He played football for Louisiana Tech University in Ruston, Louisiana. His strong arm and crafty play calling attracted the attention of NFL scouts. In 1970, the Steelers chose Bradshaw as their number one draft pick. After a 14-year career with the Steelers, Bradshaw retired from football in 1983. He was inducted into the Pro Football Hall of Fame in 1989. He has since become a popular sports announcer and football analyst.

**Ellen DeGeneres** (1958- ) is a popular talk show host, comedian, actress, writer, and television producer. She was born and grew up in Metairie, Louisiana. After working as a waitress and house painter, she began performing stand-up in small New Orleans comedy clubs. She started touring the country. She wound up in Los Angeles, California, in the 1980s, where she starred in film and television productions. She began hosting her current talk show, *The Ellen DeGeneres Show*, in 2003. Known for her wit on stage, DeGeneres also voice acts, most famously as Dory in *Finding Nemo*. In 2011, she was named United States Special Envoy for Global AIDS Awareness. She has won many Emmy and People's Choice Awards, including the Favorite Humanitarian Award in 2016.

**George Washington Cable** (1844-1925) was a Southern novelist whose writing showed the mistreatment of African Americans during the years following the Civil War. Much of his writing centered on the hard lives of Louisiana mixed-race families and the racism they endured. Cable and his friend, writer Mark Twain, often went on speaking tours together. Cable was born in New Orleans, Louisiana.

**Huey Long** (1893-1935) was one of the most influential politicians in Louisiana history. Born in Winnfield, Louisiana, he served as governor from 1928-1932, and as a United States senator from 1932-1935. Elected as a populist, he spent tax money on schools, hospitals, roadways, and other public works in order to stimulate the economy.

# CITIES

**New Orleans** is a busy port city. It is situated along the banks of the Mississippi River. Founded in 1718, today it is Louisiana's largest city. Its population is 384,320. Nicknamed "The Big Easy," New Orleans is famous for its annual Mardi Gras celebration. People also flock to the city to enjoy its historical buildings, great food, and jazz music. The city was devastated by Hurricane Katrina in 2005, but it is slowly being rebuilt. The Port of New Orleans is one of the busiest in the United States, thanks to its location close to the Gulf of Mexico. Other important industries include health care, construction, education, and tourism. Favorite destinations include strolling the shop-lined streets of the French Quarter, the National WWII Museum, and Preservation Hall, where visitors can listen to live jazz performances nightly.

**Baton Rouge** is the capital of Louisiana. Its population is 228,895, making it the state's second-largest city. It is located along the Mississippi River. Like New Orleans, Baton Rouge is a major transportation center. First settled in 1718, its name is French for "red pole," which was used to mark the boundary between two local Native American tribes. Today, the city enjoys a strong economy. In addition to shipping, other important industries include oil and natural gas refining and processing, education, and health care. Louisiana State University enrolls more than 31,000 students. The Louisiana Art & Science Museum includes art galleries, a two-story planet tower, and an ancient Egypt exhibit. The Baton Rouge Symphony Orchestra was founded in 1947. It is the oldest professional orchestra in Louisiana.

**Shreveport** is Louisiana's third-largest city. Its population is 198,242. Nicknamed "The Port City," it is located along the shores of the Red River in the northwest corner of the state. The city was founded in 1836 as a trade center. Today, important industries include retail, services, health care, tourism, and riverboat gambling. Nearby Barksdale Air Force Base is the city's largest employer. Shreveport has several performing arts centers, including the Academy of Children's Theatre, the Louisiana Dance Theatre, the Shreveport Opera, and the Shreveport Symphony Orchestra. The Highland Jazz & Blues Festival takes place each year in the city's historic Columbia Park.

**Lafayette** lies along the banks of the Vermilion River in south-central Louisiana. It is the state's fourth-largest city. Its population is 126,066. Founded in 1821, the city's motto is "The Heart of Cajun Country." Creole culture is also a strong influence. Once an agricultural center, Lafayette today relies on education, manufacturing, retail, energy, and health care.

**Lake Charles** is Louisiana's fifth-largest city. Its population is 74,889. It is located in the southwestern part of the state. Like neighboring Lafayette, the city is heavily influenced by Cajun culture. Important industries include oil refining, tourism, and education. Known as the "Festival Capital of Louisiana," the city hosts more than 75 festivals and fairs each year.

# TRANSPORTATION

Louisiana's busy waterway system has long been an important way to transport goods and people. Being located along the Gulf of Mexico opens Louisiana to huge amounts of trade from other countries. Large, oceangoing cargo ships can travel up the Mississippi River all the way north to Baton Rouge. From there, smaller ships and barges transport cargo to and from dozens of states. Louisiana has more than 5,000 miles (8,047 km) of navigable waterways. More than 500 million tons (454 million metric tons) of cargo are handled each year by Louisiana's Mississippi River ports alone. The Ports of South Louisiana, New Orleans, and Greater Baton Rouge cover a combined 172 miles (277 km) along both banks of the Mississippi River.

The Port of South Louisiana handles more cargo tonnage each year than any other port in the United States. More than 4,000 oceangoing vessels and 55,000 barges use the port each year.

*A large container ship sails on the Mississippi River near New Orleans.*

*The airport in New Orleans was originally called Moisant Field, after aviation pioneer John Bevins Moisant. The name was changed to Louis Armstrong New Orleans International Airport in August 2001 to honor the jazz musician.*

After cargo is unloaded at Louisiana's ports, it can then be transported by a network of state railways and roadways. About 3,000 miles (4,828 km) of railroads crisscross the Pelican State. There are 61,427 miles (98,857 km) of public roads.

There are about 470 airports in Louisiana. Most are small. The state's busiest airport is Louis Armstrong New Orleans International Airport. It handles about 10 million passengers each year.

# NATURAL RESOURCES

Louisiana is one of the nation's top producers of oil and natural gas. Petroleum resources are found in the northwestern and southern parts of the state, and offshore in the Gulf of Mexico. Other mineral resources include salt, sulfur, clay, plus sand and gravel.

Louisiana forests cover about half of the state, approximately 13.8 million acres (5.6 million ha). Louisiana loggers harvest

*Logs await processing at a Louisiana lumber mill.*

almost one billion board feet (2.4 million cubic meters) of pine and hardwood lumber annually.

Louisiana has about 28,000 farms covering 7.9 million acres (3.2 million ha). That is 29 percent of the state's total land area. The most valuable farm crops include rice, corn, hay, cotton, wheat, sorghum, sweet potatoes, pecans, and sugar cane.

Poultry is the most valuable animal farm industry in the state. Other important animal products include beef and dairy cattle, pork, horses, sheep, and goats.

Louisiana fish farms lead the nation in producing crawfish and oysters. Other aquaculture products include catfish, alligators, crabs, and freshwater game fish.

Louisiana's commercial fishing industry is among the largest in the country. The most valuable saltwater fish caught in the Gulf of Mexico include red snappers, yellowfin tunas, black drums, king mackerels, sharks, and menhadens. Louisiana is one of the top providers of commercially fished shrimp, oysters, and crawfish.

Shrimp

# INDUSTRY

Louisiana's most valuable industry is extracting and refining petroleum, and producing oil-based products. In good years, the industry brings almost $75 billion to the state in the form of employment and taxes. About 65,000 workers are normally employed by the industry.

Louisiana has 19 working oil refineries, where crude oil is turned into gasoline, heating oil, and other petroleum products. Only Texas has more refining capacity than Louisiana.

By relying so much on petroleum, Louisiana suffers hard times when the oil industry is down. When oil prices are low, such as during economic recessions or when the world supply of oil is too high, many workers lose their jobs.

An oil refinery in St. Bernard Parish, Louisiana.

*Engineers at NASA's Michoud Assembly Facility in New Orleans work on the Orion crew module. The Orion spacecraft is being designed to carry astronauts between Earth and Mars.*

Aerospace is an important Louisiana industry. The state has a large number of skilled manufacturers and highly educated engineers. Several aircraft and helicopter companies have factories in the state. They include Boeing, Lockheed Martin, Northrop Grumman, and Bell Helicopter. NASA's Michoud Assembly Facility in New Orleans makes parts for the Orion spacecraft, plus other rockets and space transportation vehicles.

Louisiana is a major center for shipbuilding. Other important industries include construction, health care, education, information technology, and medical research. Tourism is a big part of the economy today. Visitors spend more than $10 billion each year and support tens of thousands of jobs.

# SPORTS

Louisiana hosts two major league sports teams. The New Orleans Saints play in the National Football League (NFL). They won a Super Bowl championship for the 2009 season. The New Orleans Pelicans play in the National Basketball Association (NBA).

College and high school sports are big in Louisiana, especially football and basketball. The most popular teams include the Tigers and Lady Tigers from Louisiana State University (LSU) in Baton Rouge, and the Green Wave from Tulane University in New Orleans.

One of the most-watched college sporting events is the Sugar Bowl. It has been played annually since 1935. It is played on or near New Year's Day at the Superdome in New Orleans. The Superdome has also hosted several NFL Super Bowls.

The 2016 Sugar Bowl.

*Louisiana is known as a sportsman's paradise. It is filled with rivers, lakes, swamps, and bayous. Some species of fish can reach enormous sizes, which draw many anglers to the state.*

The people of Louisiana love outdoor sports, especially fishing and hunting. Favorite game animals include deer, rabbits, turkeys, waterfowl, and even alligators. The most popular species for recreational fishing include largemouth bass, southern flounder, crappie, red snapper, and channel catfish.

For hikers and campers, Louisiana has 21 state parks. There are also many historical and recreation sites to explore. Audubon State Historic Site is where ornithologist and artist John James Audubon painted several of his bird painting masterpieces.

**SPORTS**

# ENTERTAINMENT

Louisiana is filled with entertainment, from swamp tours to museums, from historical monuments to stage plays, or simply listening to live Cajun music at small-town festivals.

The center of the Pelican State's entertainment scene is lively New Orleans. There are many famous clubs and restaurants where the best jazz in the world can be enjoyed. Many are along Bourbon Street or other swinging streets in the historic French Quarter.

For two weekends each spring, the New Orleans Jazz & Heritage Festival showcases the state's best musicians. More than 450,000 visitors sway to the rhythm of jazz, blues, Cajun, Afro-Caribbean, rock, rap, bluegrass, and other musical styles.

Macy Gray sings at the 2015 New Orleans Jazz & Heritage Festival.

New Orleans is an exciting city all year long, but it really comes alive during Carnival season. These festivities lead up to Mardi Gras, or "Fat Tuesday." It is the day before Ash Wednesday, which marks the Christian observance of Lent. Huge crowds flock to the city to witness the spectacle. There are parades with marching bands and colorful floats, outrageous costumes, and parties all night long.

New Orleans isn't the only place to find entertainment in Louisiana. Many cities have their own Mardi Gras celebrations. There are also dozens of festivals held throughout the state, with themes about state history, ethnic groups, music, art, food, crafts, and more.

A Rex Parade float in New Orleans during Mardi Gras.

# TIMELINE

**5000s** BC—First evidence of Paleo-Indians in Louisiana, the ancestors of today's Native American tribes.

HERNANDO DE SOTO

**1541**—Spanish explorer Hernando de Soto travels through Louisiana.

**1682**—French explorer René-Robert Cavelier, Sieur de La Salle claims a vast slice of North America and names it Louisiana.

**1716**—Fort St. Jean Baptiste becomes the first permanent settlement within the future state of Louisiana. It is built by the French near the present-day city of Natchitoches.

**1718**—The city of New Orleans is founded.

**1803**—France sells Louisiana Territory to the United States. The sale is called the Louisiana Purchase.

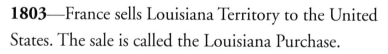

**1812**—Louisiana becomes the 18th state in the Union.

**1861**—Louisiana and other Southern states break away from the United States in order to keep slavery legal. This causes the start of the American Civil War.

**1865**—The Confederacy is defeated. Slaves are freed and the Civil War ends.

**1901**—The first successful oil well is drilled in Louisiana. It is marked as the birth of the oil industry in the state.

**1935**—The first Sugar Bowl football game is played. The final score is: Tulane University 20, Temple University 14.

**2005**—Hurricane Katrina destroys much of New Orleans. The difficult rebuilding will take many years.

**2010**—The New Orleans Saints win Super Bowl XLIV, beating the Indianapolis Colts with a score of 31-17.

**2010**—The Deepwater Horizon offshore oil spill is the biggest environmental disaster in United States history. More than 65 miles (105 km) of Louisiana shoreline is fouled by massive amounts of crude oil. Much wildlife is killed, and the state's fishing industry is hit hard.

**2015**—About 1.5 million people attend Mardi Gras celebrations in New Orleans, a big increase from the 700,000 who attended the first Mardi Gras after Hurricane Katrina.

# GLOSSARY

### ALLUVIAL PLAINS

Low, flat areas where clay, dirt, gravel, and sand have been deposited by the flooding of rivers and streams.

### BAYOU

A lowland stream or river that flows very slowly. Some marshy lakes or wetlands are also called bayous.

### CAUSEWAY

A road or pathway that is raised above low, damp, or wet ground.

### CIVIL WAR

The war fought between America's Northern and Southern states from 1861-1865. The Southern states were for slavery. They wanted to start their own country. Northern states fought against slavery and a division of the country.

### CONFEDERACY

The Confederate States of America included Louisiana and 10 other Southern states that broke away from the United States. This caused the American Civil War, which lasted from 1861 until 1865.

### CREOLE

People whose ethnic heritage is a mix of French and Spanish; or French, Spanish and African; or French, Spanish, African, and Native American.

## Deepwater Horizon

The name of an offshore oil rig about 50 miles (80 km) off the coast of Louisiana. In 2010, the oil rig exploded and sank. Oil gushed into the waters of the Gulf of Mexico for 87 days until engineers could cap the well. It becomes the largest oil spill in petroleum industry history.

## Hurricane

A violent wind storm that begins in tropical ocean waters. Hurricanes cause dangerously high tides and bring deadly waves, driving rain, and even tornadoes. Hurricanes break up and die down after moving inland.

## Levee

An earthen or concrete wall that protects low ground from being flooded by a nearby body of water.

## Mardi Gras

A festival to celebrate the arrival of Lent. Lent is the 40 days before Easter. Many Christians observe this time by not eating for one or more days. Mardi Gras takes place the day before Lent begins, which is on Ash Wednesday. Mardi Gras is an occasion to celebrate and eat lots of food. The name Mardi Gras in French means "Fat Tuesday."

## National Aeronautics and Space Administration (NASA)

A United States government agency started in 1958. NASA's goals include space exploration, as well as increasing people's understanding of Earth, our solar system, and the universe.

## Ornithology

A branch of zoology that studies birds. John James Audubon was an ornithologist who was famous for his bird paintings.

# INDEX